The Ivy Method of Learning to Read

The Ivy Method of Learning to Read

Ivy Ling Lyden

TRAFFORD
PUBLISHING

Order this book online at www.trafford.com
or email orders@trafford.com

Most Trafford titles are also available at major online book retailers.

Printed in the United States of America.

ISBN: 978-1-4269-4685-1 (sc)
ISBN: 978-1-4269-4686-8 (e)

Library of Congress Control Number: 2010918329

Trafford rev. 12/07/2010

 www.trafford.com

North America & international
toll-free: 1 888 232 4444 (USA & Canada)
phone: 250 383 6864 ♦ fax: 812 355 4082

This book is dedicated to my family

Thanks for all the help and invaluable advice from Beth P. Lyden, Kate Y. Lyden and Jane Ling Gallagher. Mostly, I would like to thank my husband, Dr. Joseph K. Lyden, for all his love and support.

Reading is so easy, a baby can do it.

When my children were young, I was looking for a guide to teach them how to read before they started kindergarten. Books that I had found were much too wordy and the instructions too confusing and complicated. I just didn't have the patience to read through a whole book and then attempt to decipher the instructions to teach my daughters. How would they be able to learn anything if I couldn't even understand the instructions to teach it to them?

Well, have you ever heard the saying "That is so easy, a baby can do it"? My teaching system is that simple. Here is my step by step guide on how to teach your reader to read the fun and easy way while building invaluable confidence along the way.

Through many years of researching different methods of learning to read and teaching pre-school, kindergarten and ESL, I have combined all the necessary tools and skills into a formula which has proven effective for anyone who wants to learn how to read easily and gain confidence while doing so. I believe that if one is well prepared, then one will possess the confidence to overcome any challenge and excel.

You and your reader are ready.

In this book I have compiled a series of lessons to help you teach your new reader. These lessons are appropriate for all new readers, starting as young as three years of age, as well as those whose first language is not English.

The success of these lessons will depend on two simple things:

1) Your consistency with reviewing these lessons with your new reader. Set aside as little as 10 minutes a day to cover a lesson or two, 4 to 5 days a week.
2) The maturity of the reader. The greater your student's attention span, the more he or she will absorb and retain per lesson.

<u>For all reading lessons, follow these three steps:</u>

1) **Point to each character (or word) and read it out loud with your reader.**
2) **Repeat step 1 until your reader can read the lesson all by herself. Patience and fun are key.**
3) **After each lesson, reward your reader with a small favorite treat or activity, reserved just for lesson time and not to be given at any other time.**

If you follow these simple steps consistently, you will be amazed by how fast your reader can read on her own, and you will be more amazed by the confidence she gains by accomplishing each lesson.

Lesson 1

1)   I love mommy.

     A   a   apple

Remember to follow the three simple steps from the introduction.

Say out loud, while pointing to the words: "I" - "love" - "mommy".

Also, when learning individual letters and their sounds:

1. Read the letter
2. Sound out its short sound
3. Stress the sound of that letter in the word that follows.

For example, in this lesson you would say: "A", "ah", "apple".

Remember to do these lessons when your reader isn't too tired. Also, your excitement level in these lessons will affect how much your reader participates and retains.

Lesson 2

1)   I love mommy.

2)   I love daddy.

      A   a   apple

      B   b   bat

The introduction of the alphabet is gradually expanded with each lesson with the focus on slowly increasing awareness and not boring repetition.

Remember to do the lessons when the reader is rested and make sure they are enjoying them.

For this lesson, you would say "A", "ah", "apple" and "B", "buh", "bat".

Lesson 3

1)   I love mommy.

2)   I love daddy.

3)   I love pizza.

     A   a   apple

     B   b   bat

     C   c   cup

Eating is always good. Pizza is popular, but you could substitute the name of one of your child's favorite foods in place of pizza.

The key here is to get your reader to start recognizing words from previous lessons as well as incorporate new words they want to learn into their lessons going forward.

Lesson 4

1)   I love pizza.

2)   I love mommy and daddy.

3)   I love pizza and mommy.

    A   a   apple

    B   b   bat

    C   c   cup

    D   d   dog

Remember to follow the three simple steps from the introduction for each lesson.

1. Point to each character (or word) and read it out loud with your reader.
2. Repeat step 1 until your reader can read the lesson all by herself.
3. After each lesson, reward your reader with a small favorite treat or activity, reserved just for lesson time and not to be given at any other time.

Lesson 5

1)   I love my daddy.

2)   I love my mommy.

3)   I love my pizza and my mommy.

A	a	apple
B	b	bat
C	c	cup
D	d	dog
E	e	egg

Remember, when reviewing alphabet letters, read the letter, sound out the short sound of that letter for your reader, and stress the sound of that letter in the word that follows.

Lesson 6

1)   I love my mommy and my daddy.

2)   I love my pizza and my mommy.

A   a   apple

B   b   bat

C   c   cup

D   d   dog

E   e   egg

F   f   fish

Don't forget to reinforce the reader's success and excitement as they learn.

Lesson 7

1) I love to eat pizza.

2) I love to eat pizza with my mommy.

3) I love to eat pizza with my daddy.

A   a   apple

B   b   bat

C   c   cat

D   d   dog

E   e   egg

F   f   fish

G   g   gift

Lesson 8

1)   I like to eat pizza with my daddy and my mommy.

2)   I like to eat pizza with my friends.

3)   I love to eat cookies with my mommy and my friends.

A	a	apple	E	e	egg
B	b	bat	F	f	fish
C	c	cat	G	g	gift
D	d	dog	H	h	hat

Lesson 9

1)   He loves to go to school.

2)   He loves to eat cookies with friends.

3)   He likes to go to school with mommy and daddy.

A   a   apple

B   b   bat

C   c   cup

D   d   dog

E   e   egg

F   f   fish

G   g   gift

H   h   hat

I   i   iguana

The reader's enjoyment is the key to success!

Lesson 10

1) She likes to go to school with mommy.

2) He loves to eat pizza with friends.

3) She likes to go to school and to eat cookies with daddy and my friends.

A	a	apple		F	f	fish
B	b	bat		G	g	gift
C	c	cup		H	h	hat
D	d	dog		I	i	iguana
E	e	egg		J	j	jet

Lesson 11

1)   We love to go to the zoo.

2)   We love to eat lunch at the zoo with friends.

3)   He and she like to eat cookies in school with daddy and mommy.

A	a	apple
B	b	bat
C	c	cup
D	d	dog
E	e	egg
F	f	fish

G	g	gift
H	h	hat
I	i	iguana
J	j	jet
K	k	kite

Lesson 12

1)   He is a big boy.

2)   She is a big girl.

3)   We are big boys and big girls.

4)   They are my big friends.

A	a	apple	G	g	gift
B	b	bat	H	h	hat
C	c	cup	I	i	iguana
D	d	dog	J	j	jet
E	e	egg	K	k	kite
F	f	fish	L	l	lemon

Lesson 13

1)   They like to go to the zoo with the big boy.

2)   He loves to play in school with friends.

3)   She is playing in the park with the cat and the dog.

A	a	apple
B	b	bat
C	c	cup
D	d	dog
E	e	egg
F	f	fish
G	g	gift

H	h	hat
I	i	iguana
J	j	jet
K	k	kite
L	l	lemon
M	m	mouse

Lesson 14

1) She is playing in school with my cat and the dog.

2) He likes to go to the park and to play with friends.

3) We are going to the zoo with the big girl and the boy.

A	a	apple	H	h	hat
B	b	bat	I	i	iguana
C	c	cup	J	j	jet
D	d	dog	K	k	kite
E	e	egg	L	l	lemon
F	f	fish	M	m	mouse
G	g	gift	N	n	net

Lesson 15

1) The dog and the little cat like to play in the park.

2) The big girl and the boy love to eat cookies at the zoo with friends.

A	a	apple
B	b	bat
C	c	cup
D	d	dog
E	e	egg
F	f	fish
G	g	gift
H	h	hat

I	i	iguana
J	j	jet
K	k	kite
L	l	lemon
M	m	mouse
N	n	net
O	o	octopus

Lesson 16

1) She likes to read books in school with friends.

2) He is playing with the cat and the little dog in the park.

3) They are eating pizza with the girl and the big boy.

A	a	apple		I	i	iguana
B	b	bat		J	j	jet
C	c	cup		K	k	kite
D	d	dog		L	l	lemon
E	e	egg		M	m	mouse
F	f	fish		N	n	net
G	g	gift		O	o	octopus
H	h	hat		P	p	pig

Lesson 17

Colors:

red	orange	yellow	green
blue	purple	black	white

A	a	apple
B	b	bat
C	c	cup
D	d	dog
E	e	egg
F	f	fish
G	g	gift
H	h	hat
I	i	iguana

J	j	jet
K	k	kite
L	l	lemon
M	m	mouse
N	n	net
O	o	octopus
P	p	pig
Q	q	queen

Lesson 18

Colors:

blue	yellow	black	orange
brown	purple	white	pink
green	violet	red	

A	a	apple	J	j	jet
B	b	bat	K	k	kite
C	c	cup	L	l	lemon
D	d	dog	M	m	mouse
E	e	egg	N	n	net
F	f	fish	O	o	octopus
G	g	gift	P	p	pig
H	h	hat	Q	q	queen
I	i	iguana	R	r	rose

Lesson 19

Colors:

blue	green	black	orange
red	brown	yellow	white
pink	purple	violet	gold
silver			

A	a	apple
B	b	bat
C	c	cup
D	d	dog
E	e	egg
F	f	fish
G	g	gift
H	h	hat
I	i	iguana
J	j	jet

K	k	kite
L	l	lemon
M	m	mouse
N	n	net
O	o	octopus
P	p	pig
Q	q	queen
R	r	rose
S	s	snake

Lesson 20

1) I like to eat red and green apples.

2) They love to go on the blue and yellow bus.

3) We are playing with the white and orange cat.

A	a	apple	K	k	kite
B	b	bat	L	l	lemon
C	c	cup	M	m	mouse
D	d	dog	N	n	net
E	e	egg	O	o	octopus
F	f	fish	P	p	pig
G	g	gift	Q	q	queen
H	h	hat	R	r	rose
I	i	iguana	S	s	snake
J	j	jet	T	t	top

Lesson 21

1) He is going to the green park and play with the big red dog.

2) She likes to play in school in her pink and purple dress.

3) They are eating cookies with the black and white zebra.

A	a	apple		L	l	lemon
B	b	bat		M	m	mouse
C	c	cup		N	n	net
D	d	dog		O	o	octopus
E	e	egg		P	p	pig
F	f	fish		Q	q	queen
G	g	gift		R	r	rose
H	h	hat		S	s	snake
I	i	iguana		T	t	top
J	j	jet		U	u	umbrella
K	k	kite				

Lesson 22

1) The boys are jumping inside the house.

2) The girl is playing with the blue fish outside the house.

3) The pink pig likes to eat green peas and yellow cheese.

A	a	apple	L	l	lemon
B	b	bat	M	m	mouse
C	c	cup	N	n	net
D	d	dog	O	o	octopus
E	e	egg	P	p	pig
F	f	fish	Q	q	queen
G	g	gift	R	r	rose
H	h	hat	S	s	snake
I	i	iguana	T	t	top
J	j	jet	U	u	umbrella
K	k	kite	V	v	violin

Lesson 23

1) You are my best friend.

2) You love to read a funny book with your brother.

3) The girl and her sister like to read books in the library.

A	a	apple
B	b	bat
C	c	cup
D	d	dog
E	e	egg
F	f	fish
G	g	gift
H	h	hat
I	i	iguana
J	j	jet
K	k	kite
L	l	lemon

M	m	mouse
N	n	net
O	o	octopus
P	p	pig
Q	q	queen
R	r	rose
S	s	snake
T	t	top
U	u	umbrella
V	v	violin
W	w	wagon

Lesson 24

1) She is going to school on a purple school bus with her friends.

2) He likes to eat ice cream with his brother and his sister.

A	a	apple	M	m	mouse
B	b	bat	N	n	net
C	c	cup	O	o	octopus
D	d	dog	P	p	pig
E	e	egg	Q	q	queen
F	f	fish	R	r	rose
G	g	gift	S	s	snake
H	h	hat	T	t	top
I	i	iguana	U	u	umbrella
J	j	jet	V	v	violin
K	k	kite	W	w	wagon
L	l	lemon	X	x	xylophone

Lesson 25

Days of the week:

Sunday   Monday   Tuesday   Wednesday

Thursday   Friday   Saturday

A	a	apple		N	n	net
B	b	bat		O	o	octopus
C	c	cup		P	p	pig
D	d	dog		Q	q	queen
E	e	egg		R	r	rose
F	f	fish		S	s	snake
G	g	gift		T	t	top
H	h	hat		U	u	umbrella
I	i	iguana		V	v	violin
J	j	jet		W	w	wagon
K	k	kite		X	x	xylophone
L	l	lemon		Y	y	yo-yo
M	m	mouse				

Lesson 26

Days of the week:

Tuesday	Friday	Sunday	Thursday
Monday	Sunday	Wednesday	

A	a	apple	N	n	net
B	b	bat	O	o	octopus
C	c	cup	P	p	pig
D	d	dog	Q	q	queen
E	e	egg	R	r	rose
F	f	fish	S	s	snake
G	g	gift	T	t	top
H	h	hat	U	u	umbrella
I	i	iguana	V	v	violin
J	j	jet	W	w	wagon
K	k	kite	X	x	xylophone
L	l	lemon	Y	y	yo-yo
M	m	mouse	Z	z	zipper

Lesson 27

1)   A big dog and a little cat are eating pizza at the zoo.

2)   The boys and the girls are reading funny books in the library with friends.

A	a	apple	N	n	net
B	b	bat	O	o	octopus
C	c	cup	P	p	pig
D	d	dog	Q	q	queen
E	e	egg	R	r	rose
F	f	fish	S	s	snake
G	g	gift	T	t	top
H	h	hat	U	u	umbrella
I	i	iguana	V	v	violin
J	j	jet	W	w	wagon
K	k	kite	X	x	xylophone
L	l	lemon	Y	y	yo-yo
M	m	mouse	Z	z	zipper

Lesson 28

1)   My mommy and the cat like to eat blue ice cream on Wednesday and Friday.

2)   All the pink and purple fish are in school on Monday and Tuesday.

A	a	apple		N	n	net
B	b	bat		O	o	octopus
C	c	cup		P	p	pig
D	d	dog		Q	q	queen
E	e	egg		R	r	rose
F	f	fish		S	s	snake
G	g	gift		T	t	top
H	h	hat		U	u	umbrella
I	i	iguana		V	v	violin
J	j	jet		W	w	wagon
K	k	kite		X	x	xylophone
L	l	lemon		Y	y	yo-yo
M	m	mouse		Z	z	zipper

Lesson 29

1) The red and black dog and the blue and green cat are going to play in the park on Tuesday.

2) The orange and white cat is eating a yellow and silver fish on Saturday.

3) The purple and gold elephant likes to read books in the library on Thursday and Wednesday.

A	a	H	h	O	o	V	v
B	b	I	i	P	p	W	w
C	c	J	j	Q	q	X	x
D	d	K	k	R	r	Y	y
E	e	L	l	S	s	Z	z
F	f	M	m	T	t		
G	g	N	n	U	u		

Have your reader read each letter and its sound.

Lesson 30

1)   The girl is flying the kite very high with her mother and her father.

2)   The bird is eating a cookie in the park with its brother and its sister.

A a	H h	O o	V v
B b	I i	P p	W w
C c	J j	Q q	X x
D d	K k	R r	Y y
E e	L l	S s	Z z
F f	M m	T t	
G g	N n	U u	

Continue to have your reader read each letter and its sound.

Lesson 31

at	bat	cat	fat	hat
	mat	pat	rat	sat

an	ban	can	van	fan
	man	pan	ran	tan

ad	bad	had	lad	mad
	sad	dad	tad	cad

A – Z   (Recite all the letters from A to Z and their sounds as in Lesson 30.)

Three easy steps to sounding out a word:

1) Sound out the short sound of "a" (ah) and the short sound of "t" (tuh) two or three times, and then say the word "at".
2) Sound out the short sounds of "b" (buh), "a" (ah) and "t" (tuh) two or three times, and then say the word "bat".
3) Repeat previous steps with all the words in the lesson.

Lesson 32

ed	bed	fed	led	Ted
	Ned	red	ked	med

et	wet	get	jet	let
	met	net	pet	set

en	Ben	den	hen	pen
	ten	men	Zen	Jen

A – Z   (Recite all the letters from A to Z and their sounds as in Lesson 30.)

Have your reader sound out each letter two or three times, and then say each word.

Lesson 33

it	bit	fit	hit	kit
	lit	pit	sit	wit

ig	big	dig	fig	gig
	jig	pig	wig	rig

in	bin	din	fin	gin
	kin	pin	win	tin

A – Z   (recite all the letters from A to Z and their sounds)

1)   The big fat pig can dig a pit to sit in.

2)   You can win if the pin made of tin is hit by a fig.

Lesson 34

ot	cot	dot	got	hot
	lot	not	pot	tot

op	cop	hop	mop	pop
	top	sop	dop	fop

og	bog	dog	fog	hog
	jog	log	cog	tog

A – Z (recite all the letters from A to Z and their sounds)

1)   The cop can jog in the fog to get to the log cabin.

2)   The fat hog got a mop to wash the dot on his pot.

3)   The tot and his dog were not allowed on the cot.

Lesson 35

ut	but	cut	gut	hut
	nut	rut	jut	tut

ug	bug	dug	hug	jug
	mug	rug	tug	lug

ub	cub	hub	pub	rub
	sub	tub	bub	dub

A – Z   (recite all the letters from A to Z and their sounds)

1)   The wet cub is in the hot tub.

2)   The bed bug dug into the rug.

Lesson 36

Review short vowel sounds:

| <u>at</u> | bat | cat | fat | hat |
| | mat | pat | rat | sat |

| <u>et</u> | bet | get | jet | let |
| | pet | set | wet | yet |

| <u>it</u> | bit | fit | hit | kit |
| | lit | pit | sit | wit |

| <u>ot</u> | cot | dot | got | hot |
| | lot | not | pot | tot |

| <u>ut</u> | but | cut | gut | hut |
| | nut | rut | jut | tut |

1) Review this lesson and any previous lessons as many times as necessary until your reader is comfortable with the short vowel sounds.
2) Start reading with your reader with phonics or beginners children's books that he or she finds enjoyable.

Lesson 37

Ending sound practice:

<u>all</u>   ball   call   fall   hall

                    mall   tall   wall   gall

<u>ill</u>   bill   dill   fill   hill

                    mill   pill   sill   till

<u>ing</u>   ding   king   ping   ring

                    sing   wing   ling   zing

Lesson 38

More ending sound practice:

<u>and</u>	band	hand	land	sand
	stand	grand	brand	rand

<u>ent</u>	cent	rent	sent	went
	tent	vent	bent	lent

<u>un</u>	bun	fun	nun	run
	sun	spun	dun	gun

<u>am</u>	clam	dam	ham	jam
	ram	Sam	slam	yam

Don't forget to continue reading and to check for comprehension!

Lesson 39

Have your reader sound out the following words:

Short "a" sound

cat	fat	mad	am	an	bag
bat	sad	rag	man	pat	pass
tan	add	fast	sank	glad	and
lamp	back	grand	tax	can	had
last	land	flag	trap	brag	black
stand	slam	than	clam	sand	has

Short "e" sound

jet	bed	set	beg	sled	egg
bed	wet	get	pen	leg	west
end	step	web	chest	vet	peg
men	desk	pest	elf	spend	slept

Lesson 40

Short "i" sound

six	rib	fit	big	kid	thick
milk	link	bib	slip	grin	ring
pick	dim	sit	lick	win	slim
sick	pink	silk	his	mix	fig

Short "o" sound

got	not	hog	dog	pop	shop
hot	hop	stop	on	lost	spot
off	ox	top	chop	pot	box
clock	drop	plot	slot	flop	Bob

Lesson 41

<u>Short "u" sound</u>

tug	bud	run	pup	fun	cut
sun	up	cup	tub	rug	us
but	club	cub	gust	pump	trust
hunt	drum	slug	mug	under	bug

Keep reading!

Lesson 42

Review any lessons you need and to reinforce what the reader has learned.

Continue to have your reader to sound out words and read simple books.

Lesson 43

Learning long vowel sounds:

Long "a" sound- with "e" at the end of the word.
The words gate and cake have the long "a" sound.

Short "a" sound	Long "a" sound
gat	gate
lat	late
fat	fate
mak	make
mad	made
rak	rake
mat	mate
rat	rate
bak	bake
tak	take
at	ate
lak	lake
cak	cake
man	mane
can	cane

Lesson 44

Long "a" sound- with ai and ay in the word.
The words rain and play have the long "a" sound.

<u>ai</u>	<u>ay</u>
pain	bay
rain	day
train	hay
brain	ray
sail	play
mail	stay
snail	tray
pail	sway

Lesson 45

Review any lessons you need.

Remember that the progress of these lessons depends on the age and maturity of your reader and the frequency of these lessons being given.

Lesson 46

Long "e" sound- with ee, ie and ea in a word.
The words tree, field and meat have the long "e" sound.

ee		ea	ie
bee	beef	eat	field
tree	reef	each	tier
deed	keep	bead	pier
feed	meet	seat	yield
greed	weep	leaf	
feet	sweep	beat	
green	steep	beast	
sleep		meat	

Lesson 47

Long "i" sound- with "e" at the end of the word.
The words kite and bike have the long "i" sound.

Short "i" sound	Long "i" sound
bik	bike
hik	hike
kit	kite
lit	lite
mit	mite
sit	site
wid	wide
tid	tide

Lesson 48

Long "i" sound- with y at the end of a short word.
The words sky and fly have the long "i" sound.

cry	fly	pry	shy	spy
try	dry	fry	buy	my
why	sly	guy	sky	sty

Lesson 49

Review any lesson & Keep Reading!

Lesson 50

Long "o" sound- with "e" at the end of a word.
The words cone and robe have the long "o" sound.

Short "o" sound	Long "o" sound
con	cone
hom	home
cod	code
jok	joke
mol	mole
not	note
slop	slope
rob	robe
rop	rope

Lesson 51

Long "o" sound- with ow and oa in a word.
The words bowl and coat have the long "o" sound.

ow		oa	
low	snow	boat	moat
bowl	show	foal	soap
glow	tow	coat	toad
blow	bow	goat	toast
crow	flow	load	float
slow		loaf	

Lesson 52

Long "u" sound- with e at the end of a word.
The words cube and mule have the long "u" sound.

Short "u" sound	Long "u" sound
cub	cube
dud	dude
fus	fuse
tub	tube
rul	rule
cut	cute
us	use
rud	rude
fum	fume

Lesson 53

Review any of the lessons if your reader needs more practice.

Repetition is the key to success for your reader at this point. Repeat any lesson of which the reader is not completely sure.

Lesson 54

Review long vowel sounds:

Long "a" sound

ate	gate	late	cake	made	bake
ape	make	rate	sail	snail	pain
paint	rain	train	brain	grain	mail
way	bay	day	hay	play	say
stay	tray	may			

Long "e" sound

see	bee	tree	three	seed	feet
green	sleep	beef	weep	meet	keep
sweep	leaf	beat	east	meat	team
beads	beast	eat	each	mean	seat
yield	tier	pier	field		

Lesson 55

Long "i" sound

like	bike	bite	hike	kite	nice
mice	pipe	wide	tide	ride	pie
die	by	my	cry	dry	try
why	fly	bye	fry		

Long "o" sound

over	oval	open	note	robe	pole
rope	cone	home	code	joke	mole
slope	smoke	boat	coat	foal	load
loaf	soap	toad	toast	low	row
bowl	blow	crow	grow	glow	slow

Lesson 56

Long "u" sound

cube	fuse	tube	rude	cute
blue	fumes	mule	rule	use

Lesson 57

Review previous lessons!

Continue to have your reader to sound out words and read on his or her own with simple phonics books.

Lesson 58

7 Days of the Week

Sunday	Monday	Tuesday	Wednesday
Thursday	Friday	Saturday	

Colors

red	pink	orange	yellow	green
blue	purple	indigo	violet	gray
gold	brown	white	silver	black

Colors of the Rainbow

Roy G. Biv

red	orange	yellow	green
blue	indigo	violet	

Read anything—books, simple paragraphs, reading passages, etc—with your student. After reading, ask questions about the story to test for comprehension.

Lesson 59

1)   I can read to my mommy, daddy and to all my friends.

2)   The little cat and the big fat dog like to eat pizza.

3)   My mommy and my daddy are going to the zoo with me.

4)   The blue and pink fish swims in the lake.

5)   The black and white zebra runs in the zoo with its friends.

6)   The tall cop tells the small boy funny jokes.

7)   Red and brown leaves fell off the tall tree.

8)   My mother and I like to go to the mall on Wednesday.

9)   Bill and his father love to eat cup cakes on the school bus.

Lesson 60

10) The nice man and the bad cat go around the globe.

11) Mommy, may I have a puppy and a kitten?

12) The big fat seal swims very fast in the blue and green lake.

13) The cute kitten is feeding the little snail.

14) Ten sad elephants went on the boat.

15) October is the best month to fly kites.

16) This is the tub in that small hut.

17) The eggs of the hen are used to make this cake.

18) I like to have my purple and yellow umbrella when it rains.

19) The bird pecks a hole in the tree with its beak.

20) We eat three meals each day.

Lesson 61

21) The mean rat ate all the peas with its sharp teeth.

22) The jet, the train and the boat are very fast.

23) The dog wags its tail at the glad hog.

24) The hot sun shines on the vast land.

25) Thank you very much for coming to my party.

26) The girl and her sister drank the milk with their friends.

27) If I am good, then my mother will give me sweet cake and hot toast.

28) The brave elf hunts the bad beast under the hot sun.

29) When we sleep, we dream about what we have learned.

30) The last snow flakes have melted.

31) You can stand, jump, run or just sit.

You can create more sentences with your reader and have fun with it. Review any lessons as necessary. Continue to read with your reader.

Sight Words List

Copy sight words onto index cards, and have your reader learn a few words everyday. Remember, repetition is the key for learning sight words. Be creative and have a great time with them.

love	fish	sun	house	cat
car	cloud	tree	stop	cheese
blue	zoo	orange	yogurts	book
picture	circle	game	hello	go
triangle	play	teacher	great	small
job	black	front	low	sleep
today	back	walk	close	cold
bring	under	job	new	off
draw	sound	their	red	brown
colors	many	words	square	long
drink	few	out	end	rectangle
would	new	last	strong	could
only	full	keep	green	very
first	monkey	much	people	one
there	favorite	where	high	because
hour	brother	cow	match	sentence

Sight Words Continued

two	here	family	away	pretty
elephant	father	beginning	sister	nice
after	room	together	how	together
before	giant	read	laugh	please
smile	again	aunt	once	start
rainbow	garden	show	sticker	strawberry
mouth	taste	nose	smell	ear
eye	see	finger	touch	pool
didn't	birthday	stars	live	puzzle
opposite	same	found	noise	ice cream
years	correct	chilly	trip	summer
fall	winter	vacation	snow	between
leaf	lunch	breakfast	dinner	butterfly
correct	complete	oval	excellent	days
months	years	inside	outside	carry
telephone	chair	television	stove	computer
computer	door	scissors	glue	teapot
soap	school	girl	name	dog
open	yellow	wash	fast	short

Sight Words Continued

jump	baby	said	why	line
can't	juice	would	horse	mouth
boy	water	milk	little	hot
font	white	shapes	story	over
home	teeth	three	jungle	clock
zebra	write	mother	share	cry
uncle	thanks	hear	what	both
pear	spring	sled	meals	weeks
seasons	won't	soda	good	key
made	build	read	swim	climb

You can build on this sight word list with your reader. Write down whatever words that he or she is interested in to expand your own list.

Now, your reader is ready for a world full of wonders and information, simply by being able to read. The confidence gained will be invaluable for the rest of his or her life.

Remember
1)   Read every day consistently.
2)   Repeat lessons if needed.
3)   Reward with small treats or activities reserved only for lessons.